Business English Verbs

David Evans

Penguin Quick Guides Series Editors:
Andy Hopkins and Jocelyn Potter

PENGUIN ENGLISH

Pearson Education Limited
Edinburgh Gate
Harlow
Essex CM20 2JE, England
and Associated Companies throughout the world.

ISBN 0 582 46896 5

First published 2000
Text copyright © David Evans 2000

The moral right of the author has been asserted.

Produced for the publisher by Bluestone Press, Charlbury, UK.
Designed and typeset by White Horse Graphics, Charlbury, UK.
Illustrations by Anthony Seldon (Graham-Cameron Illustration).
Photography by Patrick Ellis.
Printed and bound in Denmark by Norhaven A/S, Viborg.

Published by Pearson Education Limited in association with
Penguin Books Ltd, both companies being subsidiaries of Pearson plc.

For a complete list of the titles available from Penguin English visit
our website at www.penguinenglish.com, or please write to your local
Pearson Education office or to: Marketing Department, Penguin Longman
Publishing, 5 Bentinck Street, London W1M 5RN.

Contents

Getting started   7

1 Staying in touch   11

On the phone   call (back) • connect • hold (on)
put through • ring (back) • return (a call) • transfer

By e-mail   attach • call up • click • delete • e-mail • forward
log on • print • save • search • undo • wipe

By post   courier • deliver • mail • receive • wrap

By fax   cancel • come through • dial • get • load • redial
run out

2 On the job   23

Job description   answer to • liaise with • manage
report to • supervise

Recruitment   apply • employ • hire • interview • take on

Career development   appraise • demote • pass over
perform • promote • train

Industrial relations   go on strike • negotiate • represent
suspend • walk out • warn

The end   dismiss • fire • lay off • make redundant • resign
retire • sack

3 Finance and structure 35

Working together   be associated • co-operate
form an alliance • merge
Getting bigger   acquire • bid for • expand • start out
swallow up • take over
Getting smaller   break up • divide • go out of business
split up • strip
Finance   fund • go bankrupt • invest • issue shares
raise money
Dealing   deal • go long • go short • hedge • trade

4 Travel 47

Tickets   book • collect • pick up • reserve
Planes   board • check in • go through • land • proceed
take off • transfer
Trains   alight • arrive • catch • depart • get off • leave
Cars   drive • hire • insure • rent • return
Hotels   check in • check out • complain • move • store

5 Socialising 59

Arrangements   arrange • drop off • expect • get back
pick up
Invitations   accept • invite • look forward
request the pleasure
Restaurants   be off • bring • charge • order • take away
Parties   greet • introduce • mix • mingle • offer • pour
Small talk   break the ice • chat • enjoy • gossip • relax

6 Meetings 71

Arrangements confirm • firm up • make a date • pencil in
set up

Formalities chair • close • exchange (business cards)
minute

Opinions interrupt • make a point • propose • put forward
state the obvious

Discussion argue • debate • discuss • talk over • thrash out

Agreement agree • compromise • disagree • hammer out
settle • summarise

7 Money matters 83

Buying and selling auction • pick up • purchase • sell off
sell out • shop around

Negotiating bargain • barter • haggle • reduce • refund

Moving money cash • credit • debit • deposit • repay
withdraw

Paying advance • cover • foot the bill • invoice • reimburse

Breaking the law bribe • defraud • fine • swindle • trick

8 Promotion 95

To market add • announce • bring out • launch • publish
release

In the shop choose • display • enquire • generate interest
promote • select

On line access • browse • download • specialise • surf • visit

Informing the public advertise • endorse • publicise recognise • sponsor

Getting feedback get feedback • give something a plug report • review • take off

9 Reporting 107

Informing describe • explain • move on • outline • present summarise

Influencing claim • define • influence • mention

Consulting advise • conclude • consult • recommend • suggest

Apologising admit • apologise • assure • confess • cover up justify

Persuading convince • demonstrate • emphasise • insist persuade

10 Production 119

The factory assemble • manufacture • package • produce put together

Research and development design • develop • experiment monitor • pilot • research

Quality check • control • inspect • remove • replace • rework

The workshop beat • bolt • repair • screw • spray • weld

The warehouse deliver • lift • put away • shift • stock

Business Verbs Index 131

Answers 159

Getting started

Why business verbs?

Do you need English in your business? Do you need a lot of special English words? Do you think to yourself – Where can I find out what these words are?

Business is about action, and many of the words associated with business are verbs. If you learn all the verbs in the *Penguin Quick Guide to Business English Verbs* you will be well on the way to communicating effectively through English in business situations. And there are two other business books in the series – *Business English Words* and *Business English Phrases*.

What's in this book?

This book contains over three hundred very useful business verbs. Each chapter presents these verbs under familiar business topic headings. The **Review** page at the end of each chapter tests your understanding. Answers to these questions are in the **Answers** section at the back of the book.

All the verbs in the book are also listed in the **Business Verbs Index**.

Why is this book called a *Quick Guide*?

Because it guides you quickly to the most important words for you. And because you

can learn all these words in a short time.
Spend ten minutes each day with this book –
and see how quickly you learn.

Here is one way of working with the book.

- Choose a relevant chapter. For example,
  Staying in touch presents important verbs
  for communicating by phone, fax, e-mail
  and post. This chapter is probably useful for
  everyone. Read the chapter. How many of
  the business verbs do you understand?
- Answer the questions in the **Review** at the
  end of the chapter. Then go to the **Answers**
  section. Were you right?
- Now go to the **Business Verbs Index**. Write
  the words in your language.

Staying
in touch

1

On the phone

No, I can't **transfer** you!

No, I'm sorry, I can't **put** you **through** to Mrs Porter. I can't **connect** you to anyone ...

No, I'm afraid you can't **hold on** ...

No, she won't **call** you **back**. She can't **ring** you **back** and nobody is going to **return** your call ...

And no, I can't **transfer** you to another line ...

Why not? Because Mrs Porter doesn't work here. In fact, nobody works here ... YOU'VE GOT THE WRONG NUMBER!

put through

connect

hold (on)

call (back)

ring (back)

return (a call)

transfer

By e-mail

attach

log on

save

click

delete

undo

search

Hi John,

I found the report that you **attached** to your e-mail when I **logged on** to my computer this morning. I thought the report was great. I wanted to keep it, so I tried to **save** it to my hard disk. Unfortunately, I **clicked** on the wrong button and I **deleted** it instead! I tried to **undo** the command, but that didn't work. So I **searched** for it, but it just wasn't there. Could you send it again?

Many thanks,

Rita

I **searched**
for it, but
it wasn't
there.

With one click of the mouse, Uncle Raymond **wiped** his entire life!

Dear Rita,

I'm pleased you liked the report – but I'm afraid it wasn't mine. Caroline wrote it and **e-mailed** it to me. I **forwarded** it to you because I thought you'd be interested. However, there's some bad news. When I tried to **call** it **up** just now I found that it had been **wiped** from *my* computer too – it was gone! But don't worry – I **printed** a copy before that happened so I'll **post** it to you.

John

e-mail

forward

call up

wipe

print

By post

Who needs e-mail? If I want to send a message to someone, I write a letter, put a stamp on it and **mail** it. It's simple and cheap.

mail

wrap

deliver

courier

receive

If I've got a package, I **wrap** it and ask the post office to **deliver** it for me. You can't do that with e-mail, can you? And if it's urgent I get a motorbike rider to **courier** it for me. Then I know for sure it will be **received** safely. So I'll stay with snail mail, thank you very much.

I'll stay with snail mail.

By fax

FAX

To: Sonia De Soto

From: Patricia O'Learey

Date: 23.12.00

Dear Sonia,

I hope this fax **comes through** successfully. I've had a terrible time trying to **get** it to you. My fax machine was **dialling** and **redialling** your number for about three hours yesterday afternoon, before I decided that I'd had enough and **cancelled** it.

What was the problem? Perhaps your machine had **run out** of paper? Or maybe you just hadn't put the paper in properly – you really should read the instructions about how to **load** it.

But, let's get down to business ...

come
through

get

dial

redial

cancel

run out

load

Review 1

A Which verbs mean the same?

wipe connect delete ring back
put through call back

B Write the missing word.

1 He's not in. Can he .... your call later?
2 I've written the report and .... it to this e-mail.
3 I'll call for a motorbike and get them to ....
   the package to you.
4 I've been trying to send this fax all morning.
   My fax machine has .... about twenty times.

C Match 1–4 with a–d.

1 click   a) a package
2 log on   b) of paper
3 run out   c) on the save button
4 wrap up   d) to a computer

On the
job

Job description

*They all **answer to** me.*

Your job is to **supervise** the six people at the front desk – you make sure they all know what they're doing and that they don't make any mistakes. You **report to** Simon, who's the head of customer services. He **manages** you and four other supervisors. He also **liaises with** the heads of the other departments so that they all know what everyone else is doing. And, of course, as I'm the boss, they all **answer to** me.

supervise

report to

manage

liaise with

answer to

Recruitment

employ

take on

hire

apply

interview

Dear Ms Zink,

Thank you for your enquiry about job vacancies. We are a small company and **employ** just six people on a full-time basis. However, we always **take on** extra staff during our busy summer months and so we are **hiring** at the moment. If you would like to **apply** for one of these temporary positions, please call me, so that we can arrange a time to **interview** you.

Yours sincerely,

Manfred Seltzer

We are a small company and **employ** just six people.

Career development

*If you are having problems, we **train** you to deal with them.*

Every year we **appraise** you – in other words, we talk to you about your work over the past year. If you're having problems, we **train** you to deal with them. If you've done well, we try to **promote** you, although competition for the top jobs is tough so you could be **passed over** for promotion even if you have done well. And, of course, if you haven't **performed** well enough, we'll probably **demote** you, because in this company only the best is good enough.

appraise

train

promote

pass over

perform

demote

Industrial relations

*I'm **warning** you.*

These discussions have taken far too long and I'm not going to **negotiate** any more. As the trade union spokesman, I **represent** over half the workers in this factory and I'm **warning** you – if the workers that you've **suspended** aren't allowed back to work by the end of the day, we'll all **go on strike**. That's right – we'll **walk out**.

negotiate

represent

warn

suspend

go on strike

walk out

The end

*You can **retire** happily at the age of sixty-five.*

NOTICE

These are the only ways that you can lose your job at this company.

- Employees who steal will be **dismissed**.
- Anyone who contradicts the boss will be **sacked**.
- Salespeople who don't meet their targets will be **fired**.
- When business is bad, the laziest workers will be **laid off**.
- And if the company goes bankrupt, everyone will be **made redundant**.
- If you don't like any of these rules, you're free to **resign** and find another job.
- But if nothing goes wrong, you have a job for life and you can **retire** happily at the age of sixty-five.

dismiss

sack

fire

lay off

make redundant

resign

retire

Review 2

A Are these words about starting or finishing a job?

take on   apply   retire   employ   resign
dismiss   hire   make redundant

B Replace the phrases in bold with one verb.

1 I am the boss so you **are responsible** to me.
2 If you work hard, you will be **given a better job**.
3 If you don't know what to do, don't worry, we will **educate** you.
4 If I don't get more money, I'll **stop working**.

C Complete the sentences with business verbs.

1 You .... your line manager.
2 Every year a manager .... your performance.
3 The management is .... with the unions about pay and conditions.

Finance
and
structure

3

Working together

*Our two companies want to **be** even more closely **associated**.*

We've been **co-operating** on a number of projects for many years and I'm delighted to say that the result is that our two companies now want to **be** even more closely **associated**. We're not just going to **form an alliance** – we've decided to **merge** and create one big successful company.

co-operate

be associated

form an alliance

merge

Getting bigger

*A multinational **swallowed up** the business.*

The end for Sycamore?

Sycamore Stores **started out** with just one shop in a small town. The owner was ambitious and wanted to **expand**, so he **acquired** a small chain of shops in the nearest city. After a few years he **took over** another company by buying over 50% of their shares. Over the next few years he **bid for** several other companies, but he never succeeded in buying them. Then last year a huge multinational decided to buy Sycamore Stores and so they just **swallowed** it **up**.

start out

expand

acquire

take over

bid for

swallow up

Getting smaller

*The corporation was **divided** in two.*

In the 1990s the Red River Corporation was one of the world's great multinationals, before it was **broken up** into smaller parts. First it was **divided** in two. One half was **split up** into a number of smaller companies. The other half was bought by a bank which **stripped** its assets – including valuable city centre properties, which were sold to a supermarket chain – and then allowed the rest to **go out of business**.

break up

divide

split up

strip

go out of business

Finance

invest

fund

raise money

issue shares

go bankrupt

Internal Memo

The truth is that our factories are much too old-fashioned – this company needs to **invest** in new machinery. But where's the money going to come from – how are we going to **fund** this? In our position, the only practical way to **raise money** is to **issue** more **shares**. And let's hope that people buy them, because if they don't we're almost certain to **go bankrupt**.

*This company needs to **invest** in new machinery.*

Dealing

deal
trade
go long
go short
hedge

She **deals** in shares. Normally she just **trades** – in other words, she buys and sells. But it's not always as simple as that. Sometimes she **goes long** – she buys shares and keeps them because she thinks their value will rise. And sometimes she sells shares that she hasn't bought yet because she thinks their value will fall – that's called **going short**. Obviously it's risky but she can always **hedge** by buying lots of different kinds of shares and hope that if one goes down another will go up.

*Sometimes she **goes long** ... and sometimes she **goes short**.*

Review 3

A Match the words with similar meanings.

trade   go out of business   split up   divide
deal   swallow up   take over   go bankrupt

B Complete these sentences with a verb.

1 The two companies have become one;
  they've ..... .
2 She's selling shares she hasn't got; she's ..... .
3 He's holding the shares because he thinks
  they'll rise; he's ..... .
4 He doesn't want to take too big a risk so he's
  going to ..... .

C Replace the words with business verbs.

1 Our company wants to **get bigger**.
2 We've been **working together** for many years.
3 They are **trying to buy** their main rival.
4 They've **bought** two new factories.

Travel

4

Tickets

*Can I **book** two seats on the three o'clock train to Hamburg?*

MAN: Can I **book** two seats on the three o'clock train to Hamburg?

WOMAN: Yes, I can **reserve** two seats for you.

MAN: Is it okay if I pay cash when I **pick** them **up**?

WOMAN: Yes, but you'll have to **collect** them at least half an hour before departure.

MAN: No problem.

book

reserve

pick up

collect

Planes

land

transfer

take off

check in

go
through

proceed

board

Right, let's check the details. Your flight from Sydney has just **landed** and you want to **transfer** to a flight to Dubai. Now, I'm afraid that you're a bit late. In fact your next plane's due to **take off** in just under twenty minutes. So when you've **checked in** this luggage, please **go through** passport control immediately and then **proceed** to gate 54 where your plane is now **boarding**.

Your next plane's due to **take off** in just under twenty minutes.

Trains

*You should **alight** at Piccadilly station, madam.*

WOMAN:	I'd like to **catch** the next train to Manchester. What time does it **leave**?	
MAN:	It **departs** at 9.27, madam.	**catch**
WOMAN:	And when does it **arrive**?	**leave**
MAN:	It depends which station you want, madam. Manchester's a big place.	**depart**
WOMAN:	Yes, of course. Well, where do I **get off** for the city centre?	**arrive** **get off**
MAN:	You should **alight** at Piccadilly station, madam.	**alight**
WOMAN:	You mean I get off at Piccadilly station?	
MAN:	That's exactly what I said, madam.	

Cars

drive
rent
hire
return
insure

Dear Angelike

The best way to get to our office is to **drive**. I can give you the phone number of a local company where you can **rent** a car cheaply or, of course, you can **hire** one from one of the big companies when you arrive at the airport. The problem with renting at the airport is that you have to **return** the car there when you've finished with it. And don't forget to **insure** the car in case you have an accident.

*Don't forget to **insure** the car in case you have an accident.*

Hotels

*Don't **complain**, just move to a more expensive hotel.*

～ Dear Guest ～

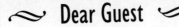

When you **check in**, we ask you to pay the full price for your room in cash. To keep our prices low, there are no porters at this hotel so you have to carry your luggage yourself. You have to **check out** by nine o'clock in the morning but you can **store** your bags in our luggage room for a fee of just £15 per day.

If you don't like the hotel's policies, don't **complain**, just **move** to a more expensive hotel!

check in

check out

store

complain

move

Review 4

A Use business verbs to fill these gaps.

1 At the airport you should .... for your
   flight, then .... passport control and .... to
   gate 24 where your plane will be .... .

2 When you .... a car you should always .... it
   in case you have an accident. You normally
   have to .... it to the rental office in the
   morning.

3 When you have .... of a hotel you can
   normally .... your bags in the luggage
   room and .... them later.

B Match the words with similar meanings.

alight	arrive	book
collect	depart	get off
hire	land	leave
pick up	rent	reserve

Socialising

5

Arrangements

arrange
pick up
expect
drop off
get back

I've **arranged** the meeting for 3.30, so I'll **pick** you **up** in my car outside the Grand Hotel at 3.15 and drive you there. Can you wait for me on the pavement just outside the main entrance?

We're only **expecting** two other people to come to the meeting so it shouldn't last too long. When we've finished I can **drop** you **off** at the hotel again, so you should **get back** to your room by 5.30 at the latest.

I'll **pick** you **up** in my car at 3.15.

Invitations

THE **GENEVA** ART GALLERY
requests the pleasure of
your company at the opening
of its
NEW EXHIBITION
" TALL SHIPS "

R.S.V.P.   6.30 TUESDAY 6 JUNE
Paul Nelson
Geneva Gallery
Compton St. SE2

482 Montague Court
London
NW1

27 May

Dear Mr Nelson,

Thank you for **inviting** me to the opening of the exhibition next Tuesday.

I am pleased to say that I am free that evening and so I am delighted to **accept**.

I **look forward** to meeting you there.

Yours sincerely,

Delphine Shaker

Delphine Shaker

request
the
pleasure

invite

accept

look
forward

Restaurants

*I'm not going to eat it, so please **take** it **away**.*

WOMAN:	Excuse me! This fish smells strange – it must **be off**.
WAITER:	It can't be, madam, it was fresh this morning.
WOMAN:	Well, I'm not going to eat it, so please **take** it **away**.
WAITER:	Of course, madam.
WOMAN:	And I hope you're not going to **charge** me for it.
WAITER:	Certainly not, madam.
WOMAN:	Good. Now **bring** me the menu again so that I can **order** something else.

be off

take away

charge

bring

order

Parties

TO THE PARTY

*Wayne always **greeted** his guests with a friendly word and a joke.*

Wayne was the perfect host. He always **greeted** his guests at the door with a friendly word and a joke. Then he would ask, 'Can I **offer** you something to eat or **pour** you a drink?'

If the guest didn't know anyone, Wayne would **introduce** them to one or two people, but he never stayed with one guest for too long. He knew it was important for a host to **mix** with everyone at a party and he liked his guests to **mingle** with each other as well.

greet

offer

pour

introduce

mix

mingle

Small talk

break
the ice

relax

chat

gossip

enjoy

People were very quiet at the start of the party, but then Norman told a funny story which **broke the ice**. Everyone **relaxed** after that and soon we were all **chatting** happily. I **gossiped** with Tina about people in the office – I never knew they had such interesting lives outside work. In the end we all **enjoyed** the party so much that we didn't want to leave.

Norman told a funny story which **broke the ice**.

Review 5

A Complete these sentences.

1 She didn't eat the chicken because it was ..... .
2 He picked her .... in his car.
3 He got .... to his office at three after lunch.
4 She dropped him .... at his flat after work.
5 I'm looking .... to meeting you next week.

B Choose the correct verb.

1 They **arranged** / **ordered** to meet the next day.
2 I'd like to **introduce** / **invite** you to my party.
3 The hostess **accepted** / **greeted** her guests.
4 They **expected** / **waited** fifty people at the reception.

C Match 1–3 with a–c.

1 request	a) the ice
2 break	b) a drink
3 pour	c) the pleasure

Meetings

6

Arrangements

*I don't know what I'm doing over the next few weeks so I can't **confirm** it now.*

A: Shall we **set up** a meeting to discuss the proposal?

B: That's a good idea.

A: Can we **make a date** for some time around the beginning of September?

B: That sounds okay, but I don't know exactly what I'm doing over the next few weeks so I can't **confirm** it now.

A: That's no problem. Let's **pencil in** a time and date, and I'll call you two days before so that we can **firm** it **up**.

set up

make a date

confirm

pencil in

firm up

Formalities

chair

exchange
(business
cards)

minute

close

Reginald was **chairing** the meeting
today, so it was very formal. At the
beginning he introduced every
single person and asked us all to
exchange business cards – which
was pointless, because we knew
each other already. Then he made
sure that his secretary **minuted**
every tiny point – the poor woman
didn't stop writing for the whole
hour. And when he **closed** the
meeting he spoke for so long that
three people fell asleep.

*Reginald was **chairing** the meeting today.*

Opinions

*Whatever you do, don't **interrupt** me when I'm talking.*

I hate people who waste my time in meetings. So if you're just going to **state the obvious**, it's probably better to keep your mouth shut. But if you really want to **make a point** about something on the agenda, if you want to **put forward** a new idea or if you want to **propose** a solution to a problem, then I'm very happy to listen. But whatever you do, don't **interrupt** me when I'm talking.

state the obvious

make a point

put forward

propose

interrupt

Discussion

discuss
talk over
debate
argue
thrash
out

We've been **discussing** the plan all afternoon. Things started quietly. First we **talked over** our roles in the project and then we **debated** the good and the bad points of the plan. Unfortunately, everybody had a different opinion on the budget, so we **argued** about that for ages. It took us over an hour just to **thrash out** a solution on that one point.

We **argued** about it for ages.

Agreement

*It takes such a long time to **hammer out** a deal.*

Okay. Let's **summarise** the position. This is what we've decided so far.

I **agree** with you on point one, that's okay.

But we **disagree** on point two, so that's still a problem.

We've **compromised** on point three – I've given a bit and so have you.

Can we please **settle** this whole thing now and go home?

It takes such a long time to **hammer out** a deal, doesn't it?

summarise

agree

disagree

compromise

settle

hammer out

Review 6

A Complete the sentences with business verbs.

1 When you have a different opinion from another person, you .... with them.

2 When you want to speak while another person is talking, you .... them.

3 When you give a little and the other person gives a little, you ..... .

B Match 1–3 with a–c.

1 chair   a) business cards

2 make   b) a date

3 exchange   c) a meeting

C Match the words with similar meanings.

argue confirm debate discuss
firm up hammer out propose
put forward talk over thrash out

Money
matters

7

Buying and selling

shop
around

sell off

purchase

pick up

sell out

auction

The World Wide Web makes it easy
for people to **shop around** for the
cheapest price by moving from one
website to another. It shouldn't take
long to find a company which is
selling things **off** cheaply. This means
that big companies can now **purchase**
their supplies more efficiently and
ordinary people can **pick up** things at
much better prices than before.

It's also easy to find what you want. If
one company has **sold out** of a

product, you can probably find it at another website. And if you're looking for something rare, visit a website which **auctions** unusual things to the buyer who pays the highest price.

If you're looking for something rare, visit a website which **auctions** unusual things.

Negotiating

bargain
haggle
reduce
barter
refund

I learnt to negotiate in our local street market. The traders all hated me because I **bargained** over everything. I knew their prices weren't fixed so I always **haggled** until they **reduced** them. When I didn't have enough money to buy something, I **bartered** – I tried to exchange something of mine for something of theirs. And if I didn't like something that I bought I always took it back and, of course, they always **refunded** my money.

WHOLE PLAICE £4

*The traders all hated me because I **bargained** over everything.*

Moving money

debit

deposit

credit

withdraw

cash

repay

A: There's a mistake in my bank statement again. They've **debited** £100 from my account for no reason.

B: What about the money you took to the bank and **deposited** last week?

A: They still haven't **credited** that to me either, so I've got no money in my account.

B: Well, why don't you transfer some money from another account?

A: But I need to **withdraw** money today. I want to go shopping.

B: You can **cash** a cheque with me, if you like.

A: Oh, thank you. I'll **repay** you as soon as I've sorted this out.

They've **debited** £100 from my account for no reason.

Paying

foot the bill

advance

cover

reimburse

invoice

I want you to go to New York to sort out a problem for me. Don't worry, I'll **foot the bill** for everything, so it won't cost you a penny.

I'll **advance** you some money now to **cover** your expenses. If you spend more than that, don't worry, I'll **reimburse** you when you get back. Please charge me the normal fee for your services and **invoice** me when you've finished the job.

I'll **advance** you some money now to cover your expenses.

Breaking the law

He tried to **bribe** a police officer by offering him a gold watch.

He's always been dishonest; he's **tricked** people out of their money all his life. He was sacked from his first job when he **swindled** one of his customers by making him pay the bill three times. He lost his second job when he **defrauded** his company of several thousand pounds which went straight into his bank account. The end came when he tried to **bribe** a police officer by offering him a gold watch. In court the judge **fined** him a large sum of money and sent him to prison for several years.

trick
swindle
defraud
bribe
fine

Review 7

A Choose the correct verbs in these sentences.

1 It was too expensive so we
auctioned / **haggled** over the price.

2 I needed cash so I **debited** / **withdrew** some
from the bank.

3 Can I **cash** / **withdraw** this cheque here?

4 I'll **cover** / **reimburse** you for your expenses
when you return.

5 It's against the law to **bribe** / **fine** a
government official.

B Complete the sentences with business verbs.

1 I want to find the best price so I'm going to
.... around.

2 We haven't got any left; we've completely ....
out.

3 You don't have to pay, I'll .... the bill.

Promotion

8

To market

The Dort GE 5000 will be officially **launched** at the start of next month.

Dort Motor Company

PRESS RELEASE

The Dort Motor Company is pleased to **announce** a new model to **add** to its range of luxury sports cars. The new car, the Dort GE 5000, will be officially **launched** at the start of next month with a big party at our central London headquarters. At the same time, we'll also be **bringing out** a new version of our successful Dort GX two seater.

For more information, see our new catalogue which will be **published** later today. The full technical specifications will be **released** later in the week.

announce

add

launch

bring out

publish

release

In the shop

It's for
my friend.

A: Can I help you, sir?

B: Yes. I'm interested in the cream that you're **displaying** in the main shop window.

A: Ah, yes. We're **promoting** that very heavily this week; as you can see, we've got pictures of it everywhere.

B: Is it **generating** a lot of **interest**?

A: Oh, yes. People have been **enquiring** about it all morning.

B: Can I see it?

A: Of course. You can **choose** from three different types and you can **select** any one of four different sizes.

display

promote

generate
interest

enquire

choose

select

On line

surf

specialise

visit

download

browse

access

Calling all music lovers!

Why waste your time **surfing** the Internet, when we can find your favourite piece of music for you in seconds? We **specialise** in finding music to suit every taste from hip hop to Humperdinck. Just **visit** our website and in a matter of seconds you'll be **downloading** files containing your favourite songs. You can also **browse** through our catalogue of over a million titles and find out more about your favourite stars by **accessing** our huge database.

Informing the public

*A famous international tennis star is **endorsing** our products.*

As you know, we're doing everything we can to **publicise** the new products. We're **advertising** them on TV and in the newspapers. A famous international tennis star is **endorsing** our products, so we've put her name on everything. We've also **sponsored** a number of local sports events, so we know that people will **recognise** our name all over the area.

publicise

advertise

endorse

sponsor

recognise

Getting feedback

report

get feedback

review

take off

give something a plug

We always knew that our new computer game would be a winner. Our market researchers **reported** an excellent response from everyone they interviewed. We also **got** excellent **feedback** from our main market – everyone was positive about it. The game was very well **reviewed** by the top computer games magazines. But sales really **took off** after a popular radio presenter **gave** the game **a plug** – he said some really good things about it on his programme.

Sales really took off after a popular radio presenter **gave** the game **a plug**.

Review 8

A Match the words with similar meanings.

browse   choose   bring out
launch   select   surf

B Complete the sentences with business verbs.

1 They .... our product a plug in a TV show last night.
2 A famous racing driver is .... our new range of casual clothes.
3 Sales .... after all the good publicity.

C Choose the correct verbs in these sentences.

1 Lots of people are **enquiring** / **reporting** about the new services.
2 You can **download** / **recognise** our files from the Internet.
3 We are **advertising** / **sponsoring** our products on TV.

Reporting

9

Informing

summarise

present

explain

describe

move on

outline

Right, let me **summarise** in just a few words what I've been saying. I began by **presenting** the company's results for the last financial year. I **explained** why these figures were rather disappointing and **described** the difficult market conditions that we are facing.

Now I'd like to **move on** to the next part of my presentation and **outline** the key points of our new company policy.

*Now I'd like to **move on** to the next part …*

Influencing

*And has anybody **mentioned** to you that your proposal is completely illegal?*

A: So you're **claiming** that this strategy is the way forward for us. Tell us how you reached this conclusion.

B: Well, first I **defined** the problem and then I tried to find the most logical solution.

A: Did anything else **influence** your decision?

B: No, of course not.

A: And has anybody **mentioned** to you that your proposal is completely illegal?

B: Ah. That could be a bit of a problem, couldn't it?

claim
define
influence
mention

Consulting

We have **concluded** that your real problem is that you never listen to anybody else.

GRIFFITH MARKETING CONSULTANTS
BIRMINGHAM, UK

Dear Mr Campbell,

When you first **consulted** us about your new marketing strategy, we were happy to **advise** you. Over the past year we have **suggested** a number of solutions to the immediate problems that your company faces. We have also **recommended** several longer term strategies.

However we have now **concluded** that your real problem is that you never listen to anybody else and for this reason we wish to end our working relationship with you.

Yours sincerely,

Patricia Griffith

consult

advise

suggest

recommend

conclude

Apologising

admit

apologise

confess

justify

cover up

assure

We **admit** that we were wrong and we **apologise** for our mistakes. Everyone in the company is sorry and the two people who were responsible have **confessed** to what happened and told us the whole story. We're not going to give you any reasons for what happened because it's not possible to **justify** our actions. But as you can see, we're not going to **cover up** our mistakes and we'd like to **assure** all our customers that something like this will never happen again.

*The two people who were responsible have **confessed** to what happened.*

Persuading

*She really **emphasised** the fact that it was easy to use.*

Nora wanted to **persuade** us to start using a new kind of software. Nobody was really interested, but she **insisted** that we listen. She did a long calculation which **demonstrated** how it could save us thousands of dollars in just a few months. She also really **emphasised** the fact that it was easy to use by repeating it over and over again. But by the end of the meeting, we still weren't **convinced**, so we didn't do anything about it.

persuade

insist

demonstrate

emphasise

convince

Review 9

A Choose the correct verbs in these sentences.

1 Are you **claiming** / **mentioning** that this will give us better results?

2 We **advise** / **consult** you to cut your costs.

3 They **insisted** / **emphasised** that they pay the bill for the meal.

B Match the verbs with similar meanings.

outline   persuade   admit   recommend
confess   convince   suggest   summarise

C Complete the sentences with business verbs.

1 When you give reasons for something that you did, you .... your actions.

2 When you say that you're sorry, you ..... .

3 When you hide something that you've done wrong, you .... it ..... .

Production

10

The factory

*It says it's **produced** in France, but that's not the whole story.*

A: So where are your products made?

B: Well, the outside of the box says that they're **produced** in France, but that's not the whole story.

A: What do you mean?

B: Well, most of the parts are **manufactured** in Taiwan.

A: And are they **assembled** in France?

B: Oh no. The parts are **put together** in a factory in Mexico.

A: So what do you do in France?

B: We **package** them in France – we put the products into their boxes – and of course our head office is there, as well.

produce

manufacture

assemble

put together

package

Research and development

develop

experiment

research

pilot

monitor

design

THE PROCESS of **developing** a new product from an idea on a piece of paper to the finished item on a supermarket shelf can take many years. Our scientists are always **experimenting** with different combinations of materials and our marketing team is always **researching** possible gaps in the market. When they have found a new product and believe that there is a market for it, we **pilot** the product by testing it in a small part of the market and **monitoring** people's reactions to it. If we get a good response we then **design** some attractive packaging and start to sell the new product around the world.

Our scientists are always **experimenting** with different combinations of materials.

Quality

If they find a problem, the product is simply thrown away.

We **control** our production process very carefully. Nothing leaves this factory until it has been **inspected** by a team of top scientists. They **check** to make sure that there are no defects in any of the products. If they find something wrong, the product has to be **reworked**. We **remove** the defective part and we **replace** it with a new one. Then our scientists check it again. If they find a problem this time, the product cannot be sold and is simply thrown away. Quality is very important to us.

control

inspect

check

rework

remove

replace

The workshop

repair
beat
weld
bolt
screw
spray

A: I've had a bit of an accident in my car. Can you **repair** it for me?

B: Let's see. We can **beat** that panel flat with a big hammer, so that's no problem. But the back is very badly damaged. We'll have to take it off and **weld** a new section onto it. We'll also have to **bolt** on a new front bumper and **screw** on a new number plate.

A: And what about the paintwork?

B: Oh, don't worry about that. We can **spray** the car any colour you like.

I've had a bit of an accident. Can you **repair** it for me?

The warehouse

I want you to **lift** all those crates up onto the top shelves.

We **stock** all the components for the factory in this warehouse, which means that we normally store over a thousand different parts here. Every time our supplier **delivers** new components, we have boxes and crates everywhere which we have to **put away** in their proper places. So I want you to **lift** all those crates up onto the top shelves. And when you've done that, you can **shift** those boxes from the front door to the back of the room. You'll soon get some muscles in this job.

stock
deliver
put away
lift
shift

Review 10

A Replace the phrases with business verbs.

1 Our products are **put into boxes** by robots.
2 Scientists often **try lots of different procedures** to find new materials.
3 Over 25% of their production has to be **put out with the rubbish**.

B Complete the sentences with business verbs.

1 To stick two pieces of metal together you .... them.
2 You paint a car by .... it.
3 A supplier .... components to a factory.

C Match the words with similar meanings.

check store manufacture remove
put together stock inspect take off
assemble produce

Business
Verbs
Index

Your language

accept /əksept/
I'm delighted to accept your invitation. _____

access /ækses/
You can access the data on our website. _____

acquire /əkwaɪə/
We've acquired three new factories. _____

add /æd/
We're adding to our range all the time. _____

admit /ədmɪt/
She admitted she was wrong. _____

advance /ədvɑːns/
He advanced me £100 for materials. _____

advertise /ædvətaɪz/
They've been advertising on TV. _____

advise /ədvaɪz/
They advised us to go to another bank. _____

agree /əgriː/
They agreed on a plan of action. _____

alight /əlaɪt/
Please alight here for the airport. _____

Your language

announce /əˈnaʊns/
They announced their marriage. _____

answer to /ˈɑːnsə tə/
I'm the boss so you answer to me. _____

apologise /əˈpɒlədʒaɪz/
We apologise for any inconvenience. _____

apply /əˈplaɪ/
He's applying for a new job. _____

appraise /əˈpreɪz/
We appraise our staff every year. _____

argue /ˈɑːgjuː/
They argued for an hour. _____

arrange /əˈreɪndʒ/
Shall we arrange a lunch soon? _____

arrive /əˈraɪv/
I'll meet you when you arrive. _____

assemble /əˈsembəl/
The cars are assembled at our factory. _____

assure /əˈʃʊə/
He assured us that he would be there. _____

Your language

attach /əˈtætʃ/
The report is attached to this e-mail. _____

auction /ˈɔːkʃən/
They auctioned the painting today. _____

bargain /ˈbɑːgɪn/
She bargained over the price. _____

barter /ˈbɑːtə/
Don't use money; you can barter. _____

be associated /biː əˈsəʊʃieɪtɪd/
We are associated with that company. _____

be off /biː ɒf/
This fish smells strange; it must be off. _____

beat /biːt/
We beat the metal flat here. _____

bid for /bɪd fə/
They bid $5 billion for the company. _____

board /bɔːd/
The plane to Paris is now boarding. _____

bolt /bəʊlt/
These two parts are bolted together. _____

Your language

book /bʊk/
Can I book two seats on the 9.45 train? _____

break the ice /breɪk ðiː aɪs/
He told a joke to break the ice. _____

break up /breɪk ʌp/
The company was broken up. _____

bribe /braɪb/
He bribed the customs officer. _____

bring /brɪŋ/
Can you bring some more wine, please? _____

bring out /brɪŋ aʊt/
They're bringing out a new product. _____

browse /braʊz/
I was browsing through their brochure. _____

call (back) /kɔːl bæk/
I'll call her back later. _____

call up /kɔːl ʌp/
I called up the document from the disk. _____

cancel /kænsəl/
I decided not to send it, so I cancelled it. _____

Your language

cash /kæʃ/
He cashed a cheque for $1000. _____

catch /kætʃ/
She's catching the next flight to Dublin. _____

chair /tʃeə/
She chairs the meeting every Tuesday. _____

charge /tʃɑːdʒ/
He charged a lot for his services. _____

chat /tʃæt/
Let's chat about your new idea. _____

check /tʃek/
We check all our products thoroughly. _____

check in /tʃek ɪn/
You need your passport to check in. _____

check out /tʃek aʊt/
You have to check out before midday. _____

choose /tʃuːz/
You can choose any colour you like. _____

claim /kleɪm/
She claimed she could do anything. _____

Your language

click /klɪk/
I clicked on the send button. _____

close /kləʊz/
He closed the meeting early. _____

collect /kəlekt/
Collect your tickets from reception. _____

come through /kʌm θruː/
Has that fax come through yet? _____

complain /kəmpleɪn/
We complained about the room. _____

compromise /kɒmprəmaɪz/
They compromised on the price. _____

conclude /kənkluːd/
He concluded by saying goodbye. _____

confess /kənfes/
I must confess – I didn't think of that. _____

confirm /kənfiːm/
She confirmed the arrangements by fax. _____

connect /kənekt/
Can you connect me to Mr Jones? _____

Your language

consult /kənsʌlt/
She consulted several people. _____

control /kəntrəʊl/
He controls the production process. _____

convince /kənvɪns/
He convinced her that she was wrong. _____

co-operate /kəʊɒpəreɪt/
We co-operate in the US market. _____

courier /kʊriə/
It was urgent so I couriered it to them. _____

cover /kʌvə/
The money didn't cover his costs. _____

cover up /kʌvər ʌp/
He tried to cover up his mistake. _____

credit /kredɪt/
£2,000 was credited to his bank account. _____

deal /diːl/
He deals in shares on the Internet. _____

debate /dɪbeɪt/
They debated the pros and cons. _____

Your language

debit /ˈdebɪt/
The bank debited $20 from his account. _____

define /dɪˈfaɪn/
You need to define the problem clearly. _____

defraud /dɪˈfrɔːd/
He defrauded his business partner. _____

delete /dɪˈliːt/
I didn't need it, so I deleted it. _____

deliver /dɪˈlɪvə/
They deliver the mail twice a day. _____

demonstrate /ˈdemənstreɪt/
They demonstrated their new product. _____

demote /dɪˈməʊt/
They demoted him after poor sales. _____

depart /dɪˈpɑːt/
The train departs at 15.00. _____

deposit /dɪˈpɒzɪt/
They deposited gold in a Swiss account. _____

describe /dɪˈskraɪb/
She described the situation very clearly. _____

Your language

design /dɪzaɪn/
All our products are designed in Italy. _____

develop /dɪveləp/
She's developing a model for Italy. _____

dial /daɪəl/
I dialled your number twice. _____

disagree /dɪsəgriː/
They disagreed about everything. _____

discuss /dɪskʌs/
Let's discuss some of these new ideas. _____

dismiss /dɪsmɪs/
He was dismissed for stealing. _____

display /dɪspleɪ/
They're displaying the new products. _____

divide /dɪvaɪd/
They divided the business into two. _____

download /daʊnləʊd/
You can download the software. _____

drive /draɪv/
You'll have to drive from the airport. _____

Your language

drop off /drɒp ɒf/
I'll drop you off at your house. _____

e-mail /iːmaɪl/
I'll e-mail you with the news. _____

emphasise /emfəsaɪz/
He emphasised the key points. _____

employ /ɪmplɔɪ/
The company only employs six people. _____

endorse /ɪndɔːs/
The French team is endorsing our car. _____

enjoy /ɪndʒɔɪ/
I enjoyed the party very much. _____

enquire /ɪnkwaɪə/
Nobody has enquired about our service. _____

exchange /ɪkstʃaɪndʒ/
We exchanged business cards. _____

expand /ɪkspænd/
The company expanded last year. _____

expect /ɪkspect/
We're expecting four more people. _____

Your language

experiment /ɪksperəmənt/
She experimented with different ideas. _____

explain /ɪkspleɪn/
They explained their new plans. _____

fine /faɪn/
The judge fined the company $10,000. _____

fire /faɪə/
She was fired after sales fell. _____

firm up /fɜːm ʌp/
We can firm up the arrangements now. _____

foot the bill /fʊt ðə bɪl/
We all had to foot the bill. _____

form an alliance /fɔːm ən əlaɪəns/
The two companies formed an alliance. _____

forward /fɔːwəd/
I'm forwarding Michael's report to you. _____

fund /fʌnd/
How are we funding the new project? _____

generate interest /dʒenəreɪt ɪntrəst/
The adverts generate interest. _____

Your language

get /get/
I tried to get the message to you.
_____

get back /get bæk/
We got back from the party at 2 am.
_____

get feedback /get fiːdbæk/
We've been getting a lot of feedback.
_____

get off /get ɒf/
Get off the train in Toulouse.
_____

give it a plug /gɪv ɪt ə plʌg/
He gave them a plug on the radio.
_____

go bankrupt /gəʊ bæŋkrʌpt/
The company went bankrupt.
_____

go long /gəʊ lɒŋ/
He went long on the dollar.
_____

go on strike /gəʊ ɒn straɪk/
They went on strike for more pay.
_____

go out of business /aʊt əv bɪznəs/
They went out of business.
_____

go short /gəʊ ʃɔːt/
She went short on sterling.
_____

Your language

go through /gəʊ θruː/
After checking in, go through customs. _____

gossip /gosəp/
We gossip about everyone in the office. _____

greet /griːt/
He greeted me with a firm handshake. _____

haggle /hægəl/
They haggled over the price for ages. _____

hammer out /hæmər aʊt/
We have to hammer out a deal today. _____

hedge /hedʒ/
He hedged his investments. _____

hire[1] /haɪə/
They're hiring people for the factory. _____

hire[2] /haɪə/
You can hire a car at the airport. _____

hold (on) /həʊld ɒn/
He's engaged. Will you hold (on)? _____

influence /ɪnfluəns/
What influenced you to do this? _____

Your language

insist /ɪnsɪst/
She insisted she was right.
_____

inspect /ɪnspekt/
We inspect the factory every week.
_____

insure /ɪnʃʊə/
You should insure all your valuables.
_____

interrupt /ɪntərʌpt/
He always interrupts other people.
_____

interview /ɪntəvjuː/
She interviewed twenty people.
_____

introduce /ɪntrədjuːs/
Let me introduce my colleagues.
_____

invest /ɪnvest/
Invest in government bonds this year.
_____

invite /ɪnvaɪt/
I've been invited to two parties.
_____

invoice /ɪnvɔɪs/
I'll invoice you for the work I've done.
_____

issue shares /ɪʃuː ʃeəz/
They're going to issue shares.
_____

Your language

justify /dʒʌstəfaɪ/
She justified her decision to leave. _____

land /lænd/
The plane will land in ten minutes. _____

launch /lɔːntʃ/
They're launching their new product. _____

lay off /leɪ ɒf/
They laid off fifty workers. _____

liaise with /lieɪz wɪθ/
My job is to liaise with our clients. _____

lift /lɪft/
Can you lift those boxes? _____

load /ləʊd/
I loaded some more paper this morning. _____

log on /lɒg ɒn/
I logged on when I got to the office. _____

look forward /lʊk fɔːwəd/
I look forward to meeting you. _____

mail /meɪl/
I'll mail the report to you immediately. _____

Your language

make a date /meɪk ə deɪt/
Shall we make a date for the meeting? _____

make a point /meɪk ə pɔɪnt/
He made a good point about sales. _____

make redundant /meɪk rɪdʌndənt/
She was made redundant last month. _____

manage /mænɪdʒ/
He manages a team of five people. _____

manufacture /mænjʊfæktʃə/
We manufacture 40 different products. _____

mention /menʃən/
He mentioned the report briefly. _____

merge /mɜːdʒ/
The two companies merged into one. _____

mingle /mɪŋgəl/
We should mingle with the other guests. _____

minute /mɪnət/
He minuted all the main points. _____

mix /mɪks/
She mixes well with everybody. _____

Your language

monitor /mɒnətə/
They're monitoring sales. _____

move /muːv/
We'd like to move to a different room. _____

move on /muːv ɒn/
Let's move on to the next section. _____

negotiate /nɪgəʊʃieɪt/
We're negotiating a new contract. _____

offer /ɒfə/
He offered her some more peanuts. _____

order /ɔːdə/
Can we order two coffees, please? _____

outline /aʊtlaɪn/
I'd like to outline the main points. _____

package /pækɪdʒ/
These products are packaged for Asia. _____

pass over /pɑːs əʊvə/
He was passed over for promotion. _____

pencil in /pensəl ɪn/
I've pencilled in the meeting for Friday. _____

Your language

perform /pəfɔːm/
He hasn't been performing well. _____

persuade /pəsweɪd/
They persuaded us to sell. _____

pick up[1] /pɪk ʌp/
He picked up three new shirts for £25. _____

pick up[2] /pɪk ʌp/
I'll pick you up outside your office. _____

pilot /paɪlət/
She's piloting her new product in Texas. _____

pour /pɔː/
Can I pour you another drink? _____

present /prezənt/
We're presenting the main points. _____

print /prɪnt/
I'll print you a copy of the memo. _____

proceed /prəsiːd/
Please proceed to gate 45. _____

produce /prədjuːs/
They produce 100 cars a day. _____

Your language

promote[1] /prəməʊt/
She was promoted to finance director. _____

promote[2] /prəməʊt/
They promote new books very well. _____

propose /prəpəʊz/
I'd like to propose two changes. _____

publicise /pʌbləsaɪz/
We're publicising a series of events. _____

publish /pʌblɪʃ/
The results will be published tomorrow. _____

purchase /pɜːtʃəs/
She purchased thousands of shares. _____

put away /pʊt əweɪ/
I've put all the tools away. _____

put forward /pʊt fɔːwəd/
She put forward an idea to save money. _____

put through /pʊt θruː/
I'll put you through to his office. _____

put together /pʊt təgeðə/
We put our products together by hand. _____

Your language

raise money /reɪz mʌni/
She's trying to raise money. _____

receive /rɪsiːv/
I received your fax yesterday. _____

recognise /rekəgnaɪz/
Everyone recognises their name. _____

recommend /rekəmend/
They recommended new procedures. _____

redial /riːdaɪəl/
The fax machine is redialling. _____

reduce /rɪdjuːs/
He reduced the price by 10%. _____

refund /riːfʌnd/
The shop refunded her money. _____

reimburse /riːɪmbɜːs/
I'll reimburse you for your expenses. _____

relax /rɪlæks/
Just relax and enjoy yourselves. _____

release /rɪliːs/
We're releasing a new product in June. _____

Your language

remove /rɪmuːv/
They'll have to remove the engine. _____

rent /rent/
You'll have to rent a car for a week. _____

repair /rɪpeə/
He tried to repair the damage. _____

repay /rɪpeɪ/
He repaid all the money that he owed. _____

replace /rɪpleɪs/
You'll have to replace the batteries. _____

report /rɪpɔːt/
She reported on the market's reaction. _____

report to /rɪpɔːt tə/
You report to your line manager. _____

represent /reprɪzent/
She represents a huge company. _____

request the pleasure /rɪkwest ðə pleʒə/
*We request the pleasure of your company.*_____

research /rɪsɜːtʃ/
We're researching a new treatment. _____

Your language

reserve /rɪzɜːv/
Can I reserve a single room? _____

resign /rɪzaɪn/
He resigned from his job. _____

retire /rɪtaɪə/
He retired after forty years. _____

return /rɪtɜːn/
Return the car before 10 am. _____

return (a call) /rɪtɜːn ə kɔːl/
I'm returning your call. _____

review /rɪvjuː/
The papers reviewed our new product. _____

rework /riːwɜːk/
They're reworking some of the figures. _____

ring (back) /rɪŋ bæk/
He rang her back that evening. _____

run out /rʌn aʊt/
The fax machine has run out of paper. _____

sack /sæk/
She sacked him because he lied to her. _____

Your language

save /seɪv/
I saved it to my hard disk.
_____

screw /skruː/
She screwed the bracket to the wall.
_____

search /sɜːtʃ/
I've searched everywhere for the file.
_____

select /sɪlekt/
Please select one of these items.
_____

sell off /sel ɒf/
They're selling off last year's stock.
_____

sell out /sel aʊt/
They've sold out of that new CD.
_____

send /send/
I sent your letter yesterday.
_____

set up /set ʌp/
We've set up a meetings for March.
_____

settle /setl/
Let's settle this matter right now.
_____

shift /ʃɪft/
He shifted the boxes to another room.
_____

Your language

shop around /ʃɒp əraʊnd/
She shops around for the best prices. _____

specialise /speʃəlaɪz/
We specialise in supplying wine. _____

split up /splɪt ʌp/
The company was split up. _____

sponsor /spɒnsə/
We sponsored the rugby team last year. _____

spray /spreɪ/
She sprayed the car with green paint. _____

start out /staːt aʊt/
She started out with $1,000. _____

state the obvious /steɪt ðiː ɒbvɪəs/
He was always stating the obvious. _____

stock /stɒk/
We stock all the spare parts. _____

store /stɔː/
Can you store it in the warehouse? _____

strip /strɪp/
They stripped the company's assets. _____

Your language

suggest /sədʒest/
We suggest a different course of action. _____

summarise /sʌməraɪz/
He summarised the main argument. _____

supervise /suːpəvaɪz/
She supervises the telephone operators. _____

surf /sɜːf/
I enjoy surfing the Internet. _____

suspend /səspend/
They suspended him from his job. _____

swallow up /swɒləʊ ʌp/
A bigger company swallowed us up. _____

swindle /swɪndl/
He swindled us out of millions. _____

take away /teɪk əweɪ/
Can you take away our plates, please? _____

take off[1] /teɪk ɒf/
The plane takes off at 7 pm. _____

take off[2] /teɪk ɒf/
Sales really took off in the summer. _____

Your language

take on /teɪk ɒn/
They take on extra staff in August. _____

take over /teɪk əʊvə/
They took us over in March. _____

talk over /tɔːk əʊvə/
They talked over the proposal. _____

thrash out /θræʃ aʊt/
We'll have to thrash out a solution. _____

trade /treɪd/
She trades in futures and options. _____

train /treɪn/
She is training to be a Web designer. _____

transfer[1] /trænsfɜː/
I'll transfer your call to Ms Hart. _____

transfer[2] /trænsfɜː/
You'll have to transfer to another plane. _____

trick /trɪk/
They were tricked into selling. _____

undo /ʌnduː/
I made a mistake, so I tried to undo it. _____

Your language

visit /vɪzɪt/
To find out more, visit our website. _____

walk out /wɔːk aʊt/
They walked out in protest. _____

warn /wɔːn/
I'm warning you – don't do it again. _____

weld /weld/
We'll weld these two panels together. _____

wipe /waɪp/
The file was wiped from the computer. _____

withdraw /wɪðdrɔː/
She withdrew all her savings. _____

wrap /ræp/
I wrapped the parcel carefully. _____

Answers

Review 1
A wipe/delete; connect/put through; ring back/call back
B 1 return 2 attached 3 courier 4 redialled
C 1c 2d 3b 4a

Review 2
A Starting – take on, apply, employ, hire
   Finishing – retire, resign, dismiss, make redundant
B 1 answer 2 promoted 3 train 4 go on strike
C 1 report to 2 appraises 3 negotiating

Review 3
A trade/deal; go out of business/go bankrupt;
   split up/divide; swallow up/take over
B 1 merged 2 going short 3 going long 4 hedge
C 1 expand 2 co-operating 3 bidding for 4 acquired

Review 4
A 1 check in/go through/proceed/boarding
   2 hire/insure/return 3 checked out/store/collect
B alight/get off; arrive/land; book/reserve; collect/pick up;
   depart/leave; hire/rent

Review 5
A 1 off 2 up 3 back 4 off 5 forward

B 1 arranged 2 invite 3 greeted 4 expected
C 1c 2a 3b

Review 6

A 1 disagree 2 interrupt 3 compromise
B 1c 2b 3a
C argue/debate; confirm/firm up; discuss/talk over;
hammer out/thrash out; propose/put forward

Review 7

A 1 haggled 2 withdrew 3 cash 4 reimburse 5 bribe
B 1 shop 2 sold 3 foot

Review 8

A browse/surf; choose/select; bring out/launch
B 1 gave 2 endorsing 3 took off
C 1 enquiring 2 download 3 advertising

Review 9

A 1 claiming 2 advise 3 insisted
B outline/summarise; persuade/convince;
admit/confess; recommend/suggest
C 1 justify 2 apologise 3 cover … up

Review 10

A 1 packed 2 experiment 3 thrown away
B 1 weld 2 spraying 3 delivers
C check/inspect; store/stock; manufacture/produce;
remove/take off; put together/assemble